P9-BZA-171

When Green Becomes Tomatoes

Poems for All Seasons
By Julie Fogliano

Pictures by Julie Morstad

A NEAL PORTER BOOK
ROARING BROOK PRESS
NEW YORK

Text copyright © 2016 by Julie Fogliano

Illustrations copyright © 2016 by Julie Morstad

A Neal Porter Book

Published by Roaring Brook Press

Roaring Brook Press is a division of Holtzbrinck Publishing Holdings Limited Partnership

175 Fifth Avenue, New York, New York 10010

The art for this book was created with gouache and pencil crayon.

mackids.com

Library of Congress Cataloging-in-Publication Data

Fogliano, Julie.

  [Poems. Selections]

  When green becomes tomatoes / by Julie Fogliano ; illustrated by Julie

Morstad. — First edition.

     pages ; cm

  "A Neal Porter book."

  Summary: "A book of poetry moving through the seasons"— Provided by

publisher.

  ISBN 978-1-59643-852-1 (hardcover)

  I. Morstad, Julie, illustrator. II. Title.

  PS3606.O4225A6 2016

  811'.6—dc23

                                                        2015004126

Roaring Brook Press books may be purchased for business or promotional use. For information

on bulk purchases please contact Macmillan Corporate and Premium Sales Department

at (800) 221-7945 x5442 or by email at specialmarkets@macmillan.com.

First edition 2016

Book design by Jennifer Browne

Printed in China by RR Donnelley Asia Printing Solutions Ltd., Dongguan City, Guangdong Province

1 3 5 7 9 10 8 6 4 2

For my parents,
with all my heart
—J.F.

For H, I, and J, again
—J.M.

Spring

march 20

from a snow-covered tree
one bird singing
each tweet poking
a tiny hole
through the edge of winter
and landing carefully
balancing gently
on the tip of spring

march 22

just like a tiny, blue hello
a crocus blooming
in the snow

march 24

what the snow left behind
was a red scarf
next to a wooden carrot
one blue mitten
a big snow shovel
a little snow shovel
and mud
and mud
and mud
and more mud
and muddy mud
and mud

march 26

shivering and huddled close
the forever rushing daffodils
wished they had waited

april 3

today
the sky was too busy sulking to rain
and the sun was exhausted from trying
and everyone
it seemed
had decided
to wear their sadness
on the outside
and even the birds
and all their singing
sounded brokenhearted
inside of all that gray

april 12

rain makes frogs hop
in a hurry

april 23

there are things that are yellow
and new
and popping up everywhere
and there are red rubber boots
with the mud on the inside
(and maybe a frog)
and everything is squishing
and everyone is soggy
but the sometimes sun
is just enough
for a robin

april 27

today
under a magnolia tree
i ran into a dachshund named paul
he was very much a sausage
with paws
and a nose
poor paul
if only he would look up
for a second
and notice the magnolias
with their pink
and their white
and their gentle flutters
he would soon realize
that it's not so bad
to be a dog
tied to a tree
in the shade
when it's springtime
and fluttering

may 6

everywhere is chirping
and now there is purple

may 10

lilac sniffing
is what to do
with a nose
when it is may
and there are lilacs
to be sniffed

may 20

"enough already"
i whispered
to the clouds
(just loud enough
for the sun to overhear
but not enough to wake the rain)
"the strawberries are furious
and i think i just heard
even the roses sigh"

june 10

i don't know much about flowers
i don't know their names
or how they like to grow
in sun or shade
in morning or night
i don't know where they began
or how they traveled
by boat or by bird
and whether or not the rain makes them shiver or bloom
but i know how they lean
and bend toward the light
wide open as if singing
their voices (silent but everywhere)
fill up the daytime
a song much more than purple
and beyond every red
a song that makes me stop and listen
and forget
and not care at all
that i don't know much
about flowers

june 15

you can taste the sunshine
and the buzzing
and the breeze
while eating berries off the bush
on berry hands
and berry knees

Summer

june 22

if you are looking for a quiet
that stretches
so far
that your ears begin to worry
do not go to the top
of a mountain in june
where it is breezy
and the sun is
more in and out than shining
because everything
at the top of a mountain
has something to say
about the breezes
and the sometimes sunshine
and the june
that is everywhere
and already leaving

june 30

if you are wondering about me
and where i could be
on a day that drips
hot and thick like honey
walk down to the river
and around the bend
to flat rocks, warm and waiting
and there i will be
and you will find me
swimming

july 5

when you are still and quietly
in the grass
just sitting
for more than the moment
between coming and going and what's next and when
but sitting, just to sit
you will find that nothing is still
out there in the grass
where everything is running
and jumping
climbing up and flying over
and everything is moving
back and forth
to and from
everything, except for the trees
who are too busy standing up
to bother

july 9

and if a firefly
should one night appear
suddenly in your bedroom
flickering you out of awake
and well into dreaming
don't forget
that even things
lost but still glowing
love a small, whispered thank you
floating somewhere
between drifting and dreams

july 10

when green becomes tomatoes
there will be sky
and sun
and possibly a cloud or two
when green becomes tomatoes
there will be leaves
and flowers tall and standing straight
and someone splashing, jumping, diving down
when green becomes tomatoes
there will be wings
and something inching, green and small
and a sweetly, tweetly chirping song
when green becomes tomatoes
there will be round
and there will be red
and there will be tomatoes
(more red than green)
(more round than seed)
(more on the vine than way deep down)
when green becomes tomatoes

july 12

soon we will go to the beach
where we will swim
and eat plums and peanut butter sandwiches
and we will think to ourselves
as we eat
on our blanket in the sand
that nothing in the world
could possibly be more delicious
than those plums
and those peanut butter sandwiches
a little bit salty
and warm from the sun

july 28

if you ever stopped
to taste a blueberry
you would know
that it's not really about the blue, at all

august 3

if you want to be sure
that you are nothing more than small
stand at the edge of the ocean
looking out

august 5

the ocean can carry
with outstretched arms, palms up and pushing forward,
treasure to the shore
for buckets and pockets
for taking home
and holding
and reminding
of hot sand and sunshine
of jumping up and diving down
of castles built and washed away
of staring out
and wondering where
some things end
and other things begin
and if there is a space in between
or just a slow and gentle fading

august 10

just one seagull flying by
water
water
green grass
sky

august 30

if you could take a bite
out of the middle of this morning
it would be sweet
and dripping
like peaches
and you would need a river
to jump in
before a bee comes along
and calls you
a flower

september 10

a star is someone else's sun
more flicker glow than blinding
a speck of light too far for bright
and too small to make a morning

Fall

september 22

i still love you sunshine and swimming and sea
and strawberries, you know that i do
but i'm ready to move on
to something that's new
so now, i am waiting for sweaters

september 25

i like it here
on this side of winter
where notebooks are new
apples are best
and freezing still feels far away
but near enough to notice

september 30

i will give you flowers
so perfect and blooming still
i will give you their pink and their purple
and i will give you butterflies
(who are anxious and already packing)
i will give you these last few raspberries
and i will give you daylight
(not all, but plenty)
if you will give me orange
and red
and leaves
that fall and sometimes twirl
just once before floating
and if you will give me a reason
for a fire
to sit by
and wait for spring

october 2

i'm too tired to think about trees
or the way the wind moves through them
i'm too tired to notice
if they are turning
and too tired to listen
to what they would say
if they could
say anything at all
i am too tired
but i am wishing
that they would wait
for me to wake up and listen
because even tired and blinking slow
i know enough
to wonder
what the trees would say
if they could

october 5

green
yellow
green
yellow
red orange brown
squirrel
squirrel
chipmunk
bird
leaf float
leaf twirl
leaf down

october 15

because they know
they cannot stay
they fade and fall
then blow away
because they know
they cannot stay
they leave
and leave
and leave

october 22

october please
get back in bed
your hands are cold
your nose is red
october please
go back to bed
your sneezing woke december

october 31

pumpkin sprout
pumpkin shoot
pumpkin leaf
pumpkin root

pumpkin vine
pumpkin growing
pumpkin wander
pumpkin going

pumpkin orange
pumpkin winding
pumpkin ready
pumpkin finding

pumpkin pick
pumpkin scoop
pumpkin seeds
pumpkin soup

pumpkin carve
pumpkin light
pumpkin glow
pumpkin night

pumpkin droop
pumpkin sink
pumpkin mush
pumpkin shrink

pumpkin toss
pumpkin out
pumpkin someday
pumpkin sprout

november 2

more silent than something
much noisier than nothing
the last leaf
when it landed
made a sort of sound
that no one knew they heard

november 17

stuck behind
a white duck walking
in the middle
of the road

white duck waddle
in the middle
white duck walking
down the road

white duck
why-dle
must you waddle
in the middle
of the road?

orange feet-le
stops to eat-le
white duck
standing in the road

stuck behind
a white duck standing
in the middle
of the road

white duck
why-dle
must you stand-le
in the middle of the road?

white duck
hears a rustle crunch-le
gray cat creeping
down the road

white wings flap-le
feet-le
run-le
white duck running down the road

stuck behind
a white duck running
in the middle
of the road

quick-le
quack-le
pond-le
back-le

no more white duck in the road

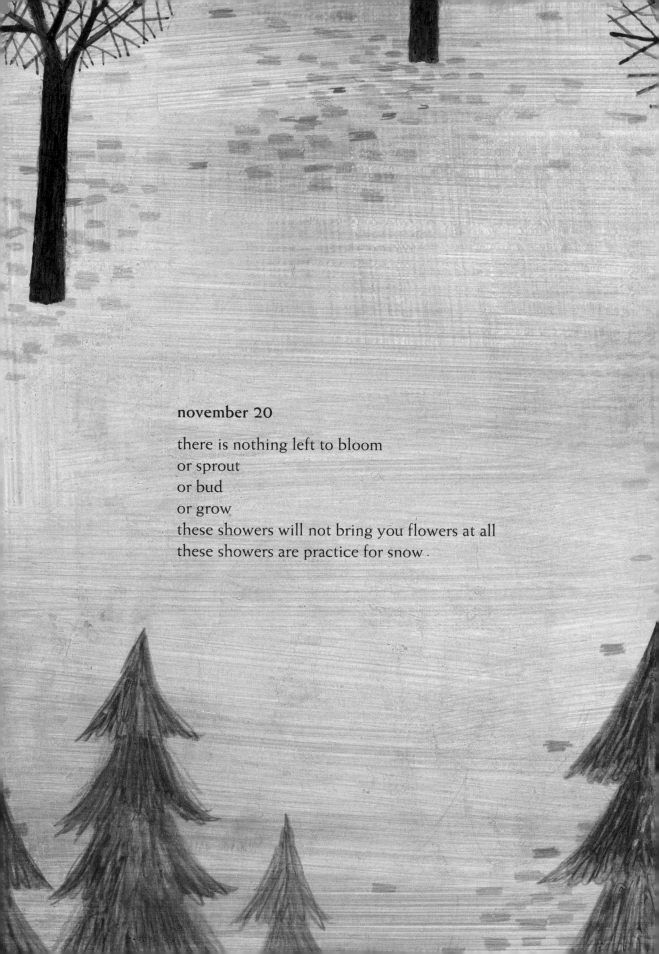

november 20

there is nothing left to bloom
or sprout
or bud
or grow
these showers will not bring you flowers at all
these showers are practice for snow .

december 11

and when the orange is gone
and the red is gone
and the pink and the yellow are gone and gone
the green that stays
is not just green
the green that stays
is cold and alone
in a forest
slightly bored
but not sad
or worried
just waiting

Winter

december 21

as if, one day, the mountain decides
to put on its white furry hat
and call it winter

december 29

and i woke
to a morning
that was quiet
and white
the first snow
(just like magic) came
on tiptoes
overnight

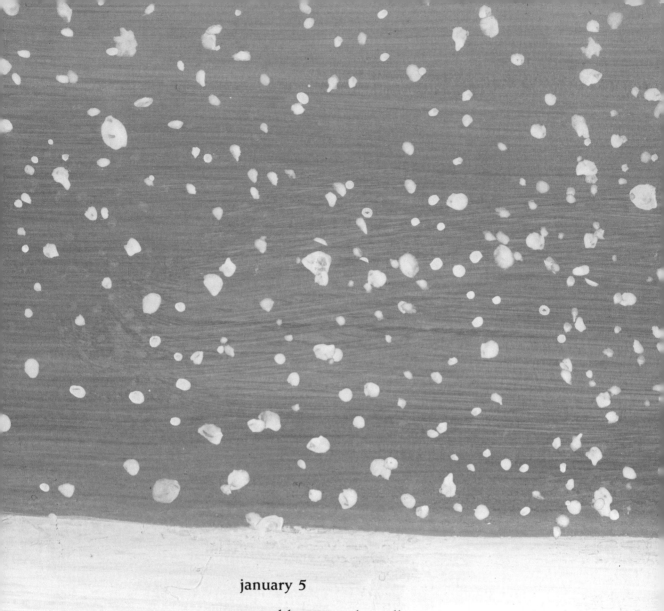

january 5

i would not mind, at all
to fall
if i could fall
like snowflakes
(more drift and swirl
than tumble thump
more gentle float
than ouch and bump)
the most perfect way of all
to fall
is to fall
and fall
like snowflakes

january 13

other than the cows
everyone has gone
either into or underneath
curled up and covered
but the cows just stand
black and blinking
not noticing that it is cold
and snowing
and everyone has gone

january 30

it is the best kind of day
when it is snowing
and the house
sounds like slippers
and sipping
and there is nowhere to go
but the kitchen
for a cookie

february 1

a gust of wind
blew by my nose
i think i will be frozen soon
this living room
(all cozy chairs and fireplace)
has some real explaining to do

february 3

with snowy arms sagging
the spruce seemed to know
that beautiful outweighs the snow

february 7

rusted and peeling
the old green bike
is suddenly beautiful
with snow on top

february 15

except for a squirrel
quick quick
and then gone
all is still
in the woods
in the winter

february 27

once there was a snowstorm
and it was big
and it was white
and it was blowing

once there was a snowstorm
and it was bigger
and it was whiter
and it blew
and it was blowing

once there was a snowstorm
and it was biggest
and it was whitest
and it was blowing-est
and blowing most
and blew
and blew
and blew

march 13

politely
but tired of mittens
i asked the winter to please tell the snow
thank you very much, but no

march 20

from a snow-covered tree
one bird singing
each tweet poking
a tiny hole
through the edge of winter
and landing carefully
balancing gently
on the tip of spring